CRAFTS FOR ALL SEASONS

MATERIALS FROM
NATURE

Important Note to Children, Parents, and Teachers
Recommended for children ages 9 and up.
Some projects in this book require cutting, painting, sewing, gluing, and the use of small materials. Young children should be supervised by an adult. Due to differing conditions, individual levels of skill, and varying tools, the publisher cannot be responsible for any injuries, losses, or other damages that may result from use of the information in this book.

Published by Blackbirch Press, Inc.
260 Amity Road
Woodbridge, CT 06525

©2000 by Blackbirch Press, Inc.
First Edition

Originally published as: *Juega con la naturaleza* by Victòria Seix; photography by Nos y Soto; illustration by Núria Giralt

Original Copyright: ©1999 Parramón Ediciones, S.A., World Rights, Published by Parramón Ediciones, S.A., Barcelona, Spain.

e-mail: staff@blackbirch.com
Web site: www.blackbirch.com

Printed in Spain

10 9 8 7 6 5 4 3 2 1

Library of Congress Cataloging-in-Publication Data
Seix, Victòria.
[Juega con la naturaleza. English]
Materials from nature / by Victòria Seix.
   p.   cm. — (Crafts for all seasons)
Includes bibliographical references and index.
Summary: Provides instructions for a variety of craft projects using such natural materials as stones, acorns, dried flowers, shells, and sticks.
ISBN 1-56711-433-4
1. Nature craft—Juvenile literature. [1. Nature craft. 2. Handicraft.]
I. Title II. Series: Crafts for all seasons (Woodbridge, Conn.)
TT160.S36713   2000   99-38940
745.5—dc21   CIP
                                          AC

Contents

✄ = *Adult supervision strongly recommended*

CRAFTS FOR ALL SEASONS
MATERIALS FROM
NATURE

BLACKBIRCH PRESS, INC.
WOODBRIDGE, CONNECTICUT

An Acorn to Be Worn

☞ YOU'LL NEED: *acorn shells, elastic cord, string, at least two colors of paint, a paint brush, and scissors.*

1. Gather acorn shells.

2. Separate the shells and break off the little stems.

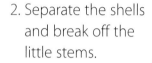

3. Ask an adult to punch a hole in each shell where it was joined to the stem.

4. Paint half the shells one color, the other half with the other color.

5. String up the shells, alternating the colors.

6. You can also make a bracelet, but use elastic cord instead of string so it can fit over your hand.

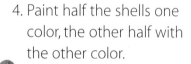

4

A Nutty Necklace ✂

☞ **YOU'LL NEED:**
peanuts, light and
dark paints, a brush,
string, and scissors.

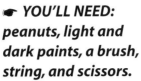

1. Ask an adult to make holes in the peanuts with a large needle.

2. Paint half the peanuts with the light color, the other half with the dark color.

3. Have an adult help you use the needle to run string through the peanuts. The string should be long enough so that the necklace fits easily over your head.

💡 *Use your imagination: What other kinds of shells would work for this purpose? What can you make by mixing shell shapes and sizes?*

5

Snag-A-Stone (A Figures Game)

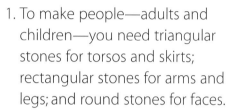

☛ **YOU'LL NEED: stones, a shoe box, and paints.**

1. To make people—adults and children—you need triangular stones for torsos and skirts; rectangular stones for arms and legs; and round stones for faces.

2. For animals, collect the following shapes:
   Horse: large, thick stones for the body and rectangular ones for the legs, tail, and head.
   Butterfly: Two triangular stones for the wings and a rectangular stone for the body.
   Crocodile: Two rectangular stones for the body and head (the wider one for the body) and four small triangular stones for the feet.

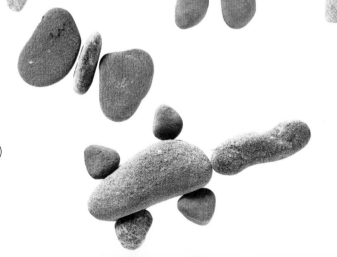

3. Wash and dry the stones thoroughly. Paint all the stones that make up a figure the same color. Pick a different color for each figure. Add details to make the figures more interesting.

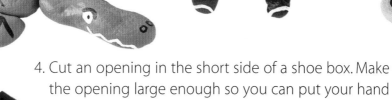

4. Cut an opening in the short side of a shoe box. Make the opening large enough so you can put your hand through it. Paint the box.

5. **The Rules of the Game:** Place all the pieces in the box and mix them up. Taking turns, each player puts a hand through the opening and, without looking, pulls out a piece. The goal is to assemble each of the figures with its proper color pieces. Players may trade pieces with each other. The winner is the player who assembles the most figures or who puts together the first one.

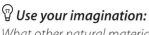

💡 *Use your imagination:*
What other natural materials could you use to assemble figures? Can you find some in this book?

A Tree-Mendous Family Tree

☛ **YOU'LL NEED: dried leaves and flowers, white glue, a brush, construction paper, and scissors.**

1. Find a passport-sized photograph of each member of your family: brothers, sisters, parents, and grandparents.

2. Place photos on construction paper. At the bottom, place your grandparents. Then put your parents on the next level. At the top, put yourself and your siblings, from oldest to youngest. Trace the outline of each photo. Draw a triangle outside the photo outlines.

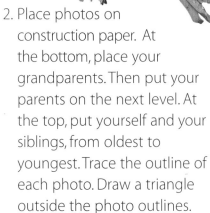

3. Cut out openings for the photos.

4. Under each opening, write how each person in the photo is related to you (e.g., *brother*, *grandfather*). Write out their full names underneath their relationship labels.

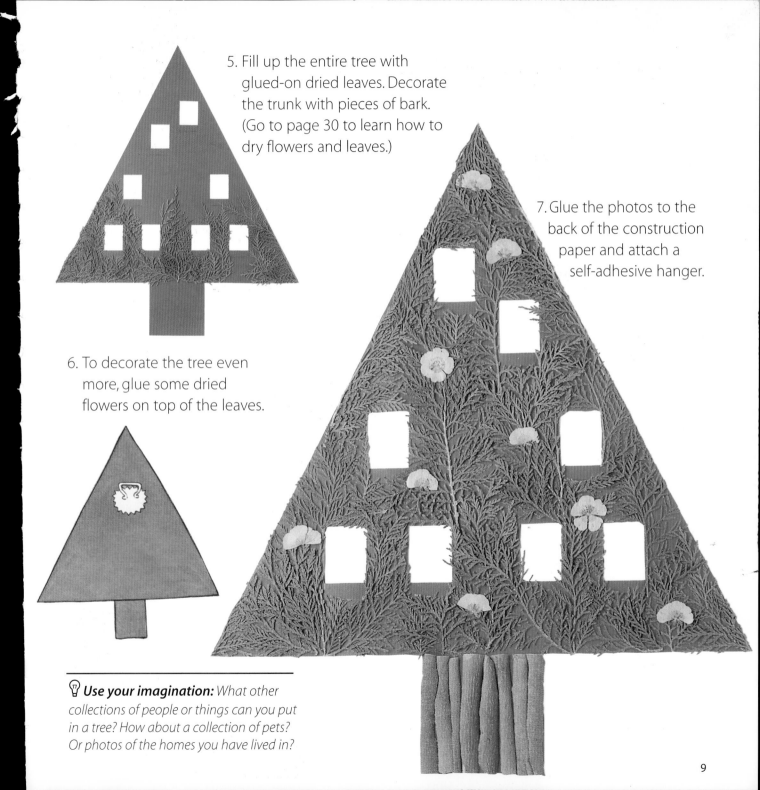

5. Fill up the entire tree with glued-on dried leaves. Decorate the trunk with pieces of bark. (Go to page 30 to learn how to dry flowers and leaves.)

7. Glue the photos to the back of the construction paper and attach a self-adhesive hanger.

6. To decorate the tree even more, glue some dried flowers on top of the leaves.

💡 **Use your imagination:** *What other collections of people or things can you put in a tree? How about a collection of pets? Or photos of the homes you have lived in?*

Fabulous Fruit Basket ✂

☞ YOU'LL NEED: stones, paints (orange, yellow, brown, green, red, and white), green modeling clay, very small sticks or stems, white glue, and a coconut.

1. Pick stones that remind you of fruit. Wash and dry them thoroughly. We've found two pears, a banana, a tangerine, and three strawberries.

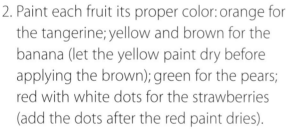

2. Paint each fruit its proper color: orange for the tangerine; yellow and brown for the banana (let the yellow paint dry before applying the brown); green for the pears; red with white dots for the strawberries (add the dots after the red paint dries).

3. Flatten a piece of green modeling clay and outline leaves on it: three large ones for the tangerine, three medium-sized ones for each pear, and a star with 6 or 7 points for each strawberry.

4. Mark stripes on the leaves.

5. Attach the leaves with a drop of glue to the top of each fruit.

6. Stick a small stem in the center.

7. Ask an adult to cut a coconut in half for you. Take out the part you can eat, clean the shell, and use the nicer half as a fruit bowl.

💡 **Use your imagination:** *What other fruit shapes can you find? Grapes? Apples? Peaches?*

Rugged Frontier Fort

☞ **YOU'LL NEED:** *a cork or cardboard mat, modeling clays (green, brown, orange, blue, and red), small twigs, two strips of ribbon, and a butter or palette knife.*

1. Cover the cork with green modeling clay. Mark out a large rectangle and press a strip of modeling clay on it. Mark a smaller square inside the rectangle.

2. Ask an adult to cut with pruning shears as many small twigs as you'll need to construct the fence. All the sticks should be the same length.

3. Add a drop of glue to the bottom of the twigs and stick them into the strip that forms the rectangle. Leave space for the door.

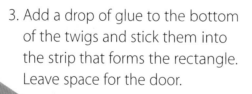

4. Glue one end of each ribbon to the twigs that make up the door. Glue the other end of the ribbons to the inside of the fence.

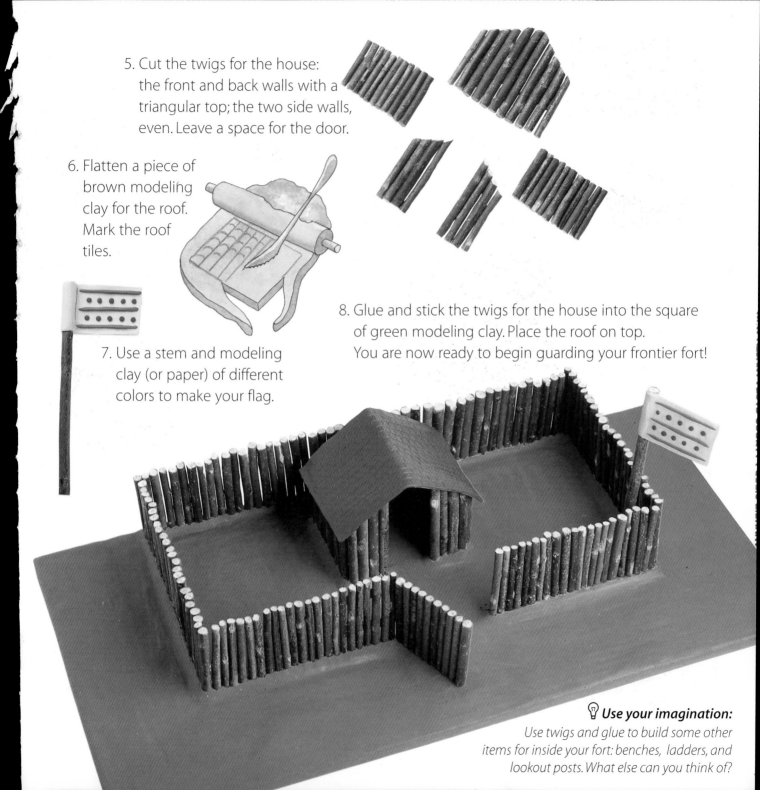

5. Cut the twigs for the house: the front and back walls with a triangular top; the two side walls, even. Leave a space for the door.

6. Flatten a piece of brown modeling clay for the roof. Mark the roof tiles.

7. Use a stem and modeling clay (or paper) of different colors to make your flag.

8. Glue and stick the twigs for the house into the square of green modeling clay. Place the roof on top. You are now ready to begin guarding your frontier fort!

💡 **Use your imagination:**
Use twigs and glue to build some other items for inside your fort: benches, ladders, and lookout posts. What else can you think of?

A Wonderful Autumn Wreath

☞ YOU'LL NEED:
black construction paper, pressed and dried leaves, flowers of different colors and sizes, white glue, and a brush.

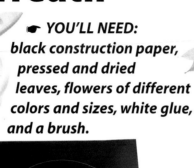

1. Draw a circle on a large sheet of black construction paper.

2. Cut out the circle.

3. Sort pressed flowers and leaves by color and size. (See page 30 to learn how to press leaves and flowers.)

4. To glue the leaves onto the construction paper circle, saturate a brush with diluted white glue and brush the back of each leaf.

5. Place the larger leaves on the outer edge of the circle. Use increasingly smaller leaves as you get closer to the center. Alternate the types and colors of the leaves.

6. To finish, select a dried flower of contrasting color and glue it to the center.

7. You can make wreaths of different sizes and combinations of leaves, petals, and flowers.

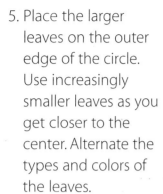

💡 **Use your imagination:** *You can use these wreaths to decorate many places in your house. You can also use them as placemats, or even for decorations on gifts and cards!*

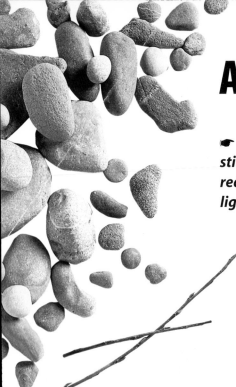

A Rockin' Zoo

☛ *YOU'LL NEED: stones, white glue, small sticks, and paints (white, black, yellow, red, brown, light brown, beige, dark green, light green, and brownish red).*

1. Look for stones of different shapes and sizes. Wash and dry them thoroughly. To form your animals, glue small stones to larger ones.

2. You can paint cats with a black base and white stripes or the other way around. Don't paint the stripes until the base dries completely.

3. To paint owls, start with the whites of the eyes, then use yellow paint for the beak and the center of the eyes. Use light brown for the stomach and eyelids, and brown for the body. Finish by painting the feathers white.

4. To paint a worm, paint each stone red, orange, brown, or any dark color. Then add white spots on the body, and paint the eyes, mouth, and antennae black.

5. To paint a dragon, make the body dark green. Use yellow, red, and light green for the crest; paint the stomach light green as well. Use black for the stomach stripes, eyes, mouth, and nose. To finish, paint the tongue red and the teeth white. Add red to the eyes and a touch of yellow for the pupils.

6. For sheep, glue on four small sticks of the same size for the legs and a shorter one for the tail. Paint the body beige and the eyes, ears, nose, and mouth black.

7. To paint a giraffe, use yellow all over, then add spots. Paint the eyes white and the mouth, nose, ears, and pupils black.

💡 **Use your imagination:** *What other animals can you add to your zoo? How would you make a gorilla, a polar bear, or a seal?*

A Super Seashell Curtain

☛ **YOU'LL NEED: washed and dried shells, a nail file, cord, and a stick.**

1. Place the shells on a table in rows of decreasing size.

2. Use the nail file to make a hole in shells that don't have one.

3. Find a stick that's longer than the width of the curtain you want to make; cut lengths of cord that are three times longer than the rows of shells.

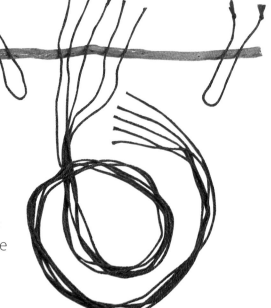

4. Use the lengths of cord to string together the rows of shells. Make double knots from the outside to the inside of each shell, so that they brush against each other and over a piece of cord on the back.

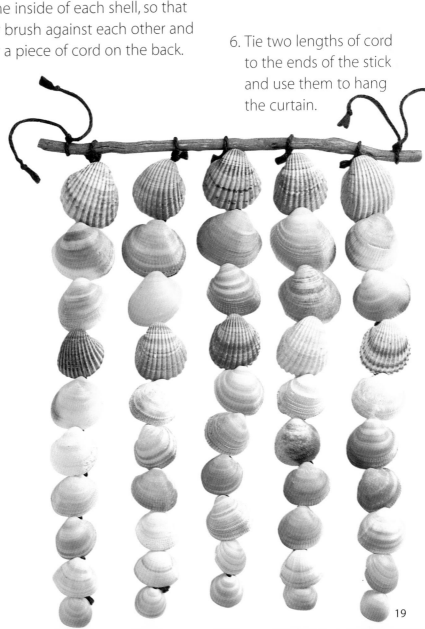

6. Tie two lengths of cord to the ends of the stick and use them to hang the curtain.

5. Tie each row to the stick.

💡 **Use your imagination:** *What else can you make by tying shells together on a string? How about wind chimes? Or a jangly decoration for a garden?*

19

A Marvelous Miniature Landscape

☞ **YOU'LL NEED: a styrofoam or cardboard tray, dried mosses (see page 30), stones, dried flowers, twigs, aluminum foil, brown and green paints, sponges, red modeling clay, glue, and brushes.**

1. Paint the tray brown.

2. Place stones in a corner to form a mountain.

3. For the river, cut a strip of aluminum foil and wrinkle it, leaving the dull side on top. Curve the strip and place it in the tray.

4. Pick pieces of different mosses and group them in the tray by textures and colors.

5. For the trees: cut a piece of sponge for the tree-top, make a cut in the center of the base of the sponge and glue in a twig for the trunk of the tree. Hold up the tree by sticking it into a small piece of modeling clay.

6. Paint the sponge green. When the paint dries, glue on fruit made of little balls of red modeling clay. Remove the clay stand and stick the tree in the moss.

7. Finish your landscape with small dried or fresh flowers.

💡 *Use your imagination:*
Can you add some animals to your landscape? How about adding a bird, sheep, or horse made from stones?

A Stony Sand Portrait

☞ **YOU'LL NEED: stones (washed and dried), sand, thin plywood, white glue, brushes, paint, and a picture hanger.**

1. Gather the stones. Use rectangular ones for the hair, the outline of the face, and the mouth; use round ones for the eyes; use triangular stones for the nose, cheeks, and ears.

hair

eyebrows

eyes

nose

lips

cheeks

ears

2. On a rectangular plywood board, arrange the stones to form a face.

3. Mark the interior outline of the face with a pencil. Remove the stones and arrange them in the same position in a safe place.

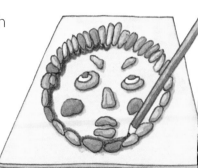

4. With a brush, apply white glue to the area of the face going a little beyond the pencil line. Sprinkle sand over the glue. Wait for the glue to dry, then turn the board over so that any unglued sand falls off.

5. Paint the part of the board outside the face area.

6. Glue the stones, one by one, onto the board to form the face.

7. Glue a picture hanger to the top of the back of the board.

💡 *Use your imagination:*
Can you make other designs with sand, glue, and stones? Try applying glue in different patterns, add sand and stones to fill it in.

An A-Mazing Maze

☛ **YOU'LL NEED: a plastic or paper plate, stones, a dried bean or popcorn kernel, colored paints, newspaper pages, adhesive tape, a toothbrush, and paint brushes.**

1. Find rectangular stones of different colors. Wash and dry them thoroughly.

2. Cover the center of the plate with a circle of folded newspaper; secure the ends of the paper with adhesive tape.

3. Place the plate on a table covered with newspaper. Dip the toothbrush in a dark colored paint and spatter the paint over the platter.

4. Let the paint dry, then spatter the platter again, this time with a lighter paint.

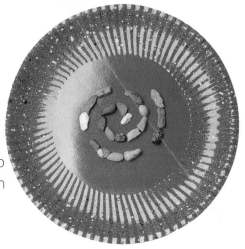

5. Glue the stones to the platter to form a spiral, leaving a space here and there.

6. If you like, paint the bean and let it dry.

7. Place the bean or popcorn kernel in your maze and try to make it go all the way through without falling out!

💡 **Use your imagination:** *Try your game with other items, such as small marbles, tin foil balls, or small coins.*

Pebble Pets and Pastries

☛ **YOU'LL NEED: paints of all colors, blue modeling clay, thick and thin brushes, and clean stones. For backgrounds, you'll need white paper, paints, a paper mat, and blue crepe paper.**

1. Look for stones with shapes that remind you of animals or objects.

2. We've found whales, piranhas, birds, and breads.

3. Start by painting bases a dark color. We painted our whales gray. After the gray paint dries, add the mouth and eyes in white. Finally, paint black lines for the teeth, eyes, fins, and tail.

4. You can make a waterspout out of blue modeling clay and attach it to the whale. On paper, paint the sea as a background.

5. To paint a piranha, first use red for the stomach, then blue for the hump, and white for the mouth and eye. Add yellow and green stripes. Add black stripes and the teeth. For the background, make a river out of blue crepe paper.

💡 **Use your imagination:** *Can you find stones for an entire banquet? How many foods can you make?*

6. For birds, paint the base in vivid colors and the spots in contrasting colors. Outline the wings, beak, and tail in black.

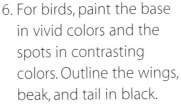

7. To make breads, paint the loaf and the roll beige and the croissant light brown. Next add the brown stripes. After the paint dries, put the breads on a paper mat.

Treasures from the Sea ✂

☛ **YOU'LL NEED:** *two colors of modeling clay, two colors of paper clips, two colors of cord, little stones, small shells, nail polish, and ready-made earring clasps.*

1. Shape modeling clay into geometric shapes to make the bases for the pendant and the earrings.

2. Ask an adult to unfold three paper clips, squeeze together one end of each clip, and cut off the other end. One clip in each set should be longer than the other two.

3. Stick a clip in the top of each piece of modeling clay. Use the longer clips in the pendants.

4. Press small shells and tiny stones of different colors into the bases.

5. Attach the earrings to the clasps and the pendant to a cord. Let the clay dry fully before wearing. For shine coat jewelry with clear nail polish.

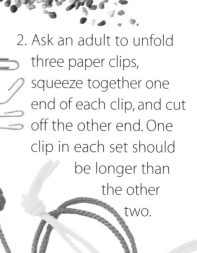

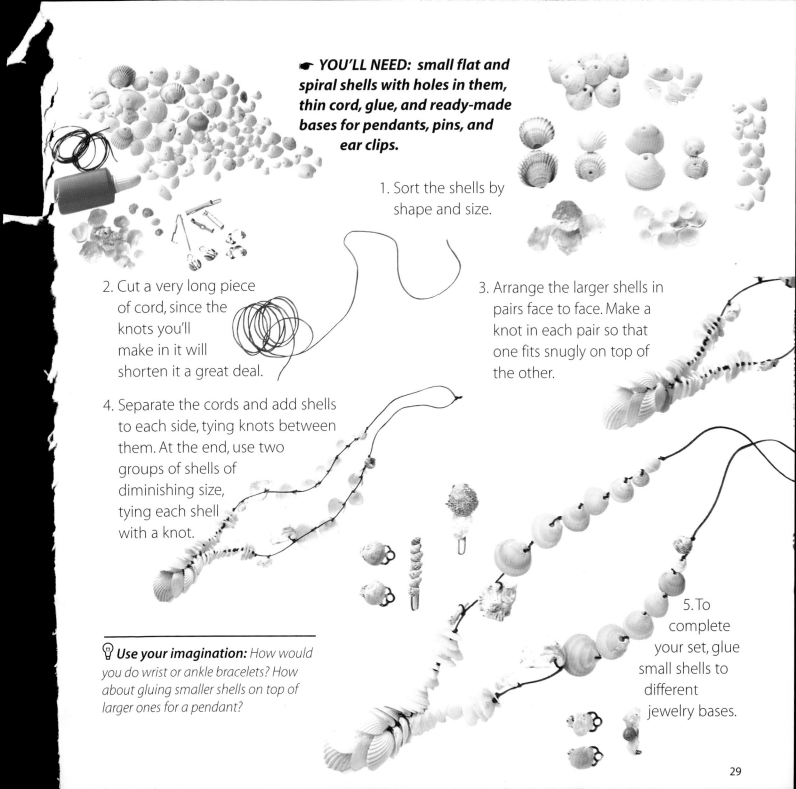

☛ **YOU'LL NEED: small flat and spiral shells with holes in them, thin cord, glue, and ready-made bases for pendants, pins, and ear clips.**

1. Sort the shells by shape and size.

2. Cut a very long piece of cord, since the knots you'll make in it will shorten it a great deal.

3. Arrange the larger shells in pairs face to face. Make a knot in each pair so that one fits snugly on top of the other.

4. Separate the cords and add shells to each side, tying knots between them. At the end, use two groups of shells of diminishing size, tying each shell with a knot.

💡 **Use your imagination:** *How would you do wrist or ankle bracelets? How about gluing smaller shells on top of larger ones for a pendant?*

5. To complete your set, glue small shells to different jewelry bases.

How to Dry Flowers

1. Gather a bunch of flowers and tie it with a string.

2. Hang the bunch up-side-down: the flowers on the bottom and the stems on top.

3. Wait a few days for the flowers to dry.

How to Dry Moss

  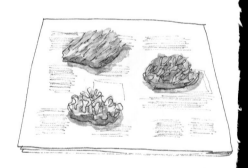

1. Pick mosses of different textures and colors.

2. Place them on sheets of newspaper.

3. The mosses will dry in a few days.

How to Press Flowers and Leaves

1. Gather leaves and flowers of different sizes and colors.

2. **Leaves.** Lay them flat between sheets of newspaper.

3. **Flowers.** Lay them flat between two sheets of white paper, then place between sheets of newspaper.

4. Place a heavy weight on top and wait a few days for the flowers and leaves to dry.

WHERE TO GET SUPPLIES

Art & Woodcrafters Supply, Inc.
www.artwoodcrafter.com
Order a catalog or browse online for many different craft supplies.

Craft Supplies
www.craftsfaironline.com/ Supplies.html
Features many different sites, each featuring products for specific hobbies.

Darice, Inc.
21160 Drake Road
Strongsville, OH 44136-6699
www.darice.com
Order a catalog or browse online for many different craft supplies.

Making Friends
www.makingfriends.com
Offers many kits and products for children's crafts.

National Artcraft
7996 Darrow Road
Twinsburg, OH 44087
www.nationalartcraft.com
This craft store features many products available through its catalog or online.

FOR MORE INFORMATION

Books

Chapman, Gillian. *Autumn* (Seasonal Crafts). Chatham, NJ: Raintree/Steck Vaughn, 1997.

Chapman, Gillian. PamRobson (Contributor). *Art From Fabric: With Projects Using Rags, Old Clothes, and Remnants.* New York, NY: Thomson Learning, 1995.

Connor, Nikki. Sarah Jean Neaves (Illustrator). *Cardboard Boxes* (Creating Crafts From). Providence, RI: Copper Beech Books, 1996.

Gordon, Lynn. *52 Great Art Projects For Kids.* San Francisco, CA: Chronicle Books, 1996.

King, Penny. Clare Roundhill (Contributor). *Animals* (Artists' Workshop). New York, NY: Crabtree Publishing, 1996.

Ross, Kathy. Sharon Lane Holm (Illustrator). *The Best Holiday Crafts Ever.* Brookfield, CT: Millbrook Publishing, 1996.

Smith, Alistair. *Big Book of Papercraft.* Newton, MA: Educational Development Center, 1996.

Videos
Blue's Clues Arts & Crafts. Nickelodeon. (1998).

Web Sites
Crafts For Kids
www.craftsforkids.miningco.com/ mbody.htm
Many different arts and crafts activities are explained in detail.

Family Crafts
www.family.go.com
Search for crafts by age group. Projects include instructions, supply list, and helpful tips.

KinderCrafts
www.EnchantedLearning.com/Crafts
Step-by-step instructions explain how to make animal, dinosaur, box, and paper crafts, plus much more.

Making Friends
www.makingfriends.com
Contains hundreds of craft ideas with detailed instructions for children ages 2 to 12, including paper dolls, summer crafts, yucky stuff, and holiday crafts.

INDEX